FORENSIC INVESTIGATIONS OF THE MAYA

Louise Spilsbury

Author: Louise Spilsbury

Editors: Sarah Eason, John Andrews, Petrice Custance, and Janine Deschenes

Proofreader and indexer: Wendy Scavuzzo

Editorial director: Kathy Middleton

Design: Paul Myerscough, Paul Oakley, and Jane McKenna

Cover design: Paul Myerscough

Photo research: Rachel Blount

Production coordinator and Prepress technician: Tammy McGarr

Print coordinator: Katherine Berti

Consultant: John Malam

Produced for Crabtree Publishing Company by Calcium Creative Ltd.

Photo Credits:
t=Top, c=Center, b=Bottom, l=Left, r=Right.

Inside: Alamy Stock Photo: David Kilpatrick: p. 5b; Arlen Chase: Courtesy of Arlen and Diane Chase, Caracol Archaeological Project: p. 9c; Shutterstock: Adalbert Dragon: p. 14; Subbotina Anna: p. 16; Bbernard: p. 10; Bonchan: p. 17br; William Cushman: p. 4; Elnur: p. 23b; EsHanPhot: p. 7; Dmitry Kalinovsky: p. 9t; Mardoz: pp. 1, 23t; Igor Marusichenko: p. 19b; Masarik: p. 6; Deborah McCague: p. 24; Dudarev Mikhail: p. 26; Tomasz Otap: p. 12; David Pegzlz: p. 15tc; Michael Rosskothen: p. 11b; Royaltystockphoto.com: p. 21; Jose Ignacio Soto: pp. 8, 29; Dani Vincek: p. 5t; Walters Art Museum: p. 22; Wikimedia Commons: Jesse Allen, NASA Earth Observatory using imagery provided courtesy of Tom Sever and Burgess Howell, Marshall Space Flight Center, and GeoEye: p. 27t; Peter Andersen: p. 25t; Authenticmaya: p. 25b; CyArk: p. 28; Durova: p. 15tl; Elelicht: p. 18; Daniel Lobo (Daquella manera): p. 11t; Henrique Matos: p. 27b; Ewen Roberts/www.flickr.com/photos/donabelandewen: p. 15b; Wolfgang Sauber: p. 17l; Theilr: p. 13; Walters Art Museum; Gift of John Bourne, 2009: p. 20; Yelkrokoyade: p. 19t.

Cover: Left from top to bottom: Shutterstock/ Michael Rosskothen; Wikimedia Commons/CyArk; Shutterstock/ Dmitry Kalinovsky; Right: Flickr/Theilr.

Library and Archives Canada Cataloguing in Publication

Spilsbury, Louise, author
Forensic investigations of the Maya / Louise Spilsbury.

(Forensic footprints of ancient worlds)
Includes index.
Issued in print and electronic formats.
ISBN 978-0-7787-4951-6 (hardcover).--
ISBN 978-0-7787-4957-8 (softcover).--
ISBN 978-1-4271-2117-2 (HTML)

I. Title.

F1435.S655 2018 j972.81'01609009 C2018-902987-0
C2018-902988-9

Library of Congress Cataloging-in-Publication Data

CIP available at the Library of Congress

Crabtree Publishing Company

www.crabtreebooks.com 1-800-387-7650

Printed in the U.S.A./092018/CG20180719

Published in Canada
Crabtree Publishing
616 Welland Ave.
St. Catharines, Ontario
L2M 5V6

Published in the United States
Crabtree Publishing
PMB 59051
350 Fifth Avenue, 59th Floor
New York, New York 10118

Published in the United Kingdom
Crabtree Publishing
Maritime House
Basin Road North, Hove
BN41 1WR

Published in Australia
Crabtree Publishing
3 Charles Street
Coburg North
VIC, 3058

CONTENTS

INVESTIGATING THE MAYA

The ancient Maya built a civilization that reached its peak around 300–900 C.E. It ruled over large parts of Central America. For many years, the lives of millions of these ancient people remained a mystery to the outside world. This was partly because trees had grown over their grand, ruined cities and hidden them deep within the rain forest.

Solving Mysteries

Some of what we know about the Maya comes from written **evidence** they left behind, such as names and numbers carved into stone. We study the **remains** of Maya buildings and **artifacts** (objects from the past) to find out more about Maya daily life. However, many artifacts are damaged and some are still hidden. Some are missing important pieces of information.

For example, there are records of rich and powerful Maya, but few to tell us about the everyday lives of ordinary people. How can we ever know how many Maya cities there were when the remains of so many of their buildings are buried beneath soil and huge trees? Is there a way to solve these and other ancient mysteries? Yes—with **forensic science**!

« The Temple of the Jaguar, in the ancient Maya city of Tikal, Guatemala, is 154 feet (47 m) tall. When the temple was built, in about 730 C.E., it was one of the tallest buildings in the world.

In the ancient Maya culture, honey from bees was used as medicine. It was also used as a sweetener in food and drinks. The Maya beekeepers' favorite kind of honey-making bee was stinger-less.

DID You Know?

Archaeologists have dug up a lot of small circular stones from the remains of Maya cities. But what were they used for? When scientists tested the soil on the stones they found tiny amounts of honey and wax. Historians believe that the stones were put at the bottom of beehives, to plug them. The stones were pulled out when people wanted to gather the honey inside. The Maya were excellent beekeepers!

HOW SCIENCE SOLVED THE PAST:

FORENSIC FOOTPRINTS

To solve crimes, forensic scientists examine evidence from the places where crimes took place, called **crime scenes**. The **techniques** that they use to solve crimes are also used by people to solve mysteries about the past. **Archaeologists** and **anthropologists** study the clues, or forensic footprints, ancient people left behind to find out more about them. Archaeologists use forensic techniques to find out about ancient buildings and **sites**. Anthropologists use forensic techniques to learn more about ancient people from their skeletons and the objects they left behind.

The Maya made beehives such as this one from wood. Bees made and stored honey in the hives. The wood can be tested by forensic scientists for traces of honey or wax.

SOLVING PAST MYSTERIES

Forensic scientists can help police find a body in a crime scene, and they can also find out where ancient bodies are buried. They dig up any items buried with the bodies, carefully make a note of them, and **preserve** them. They use forensic science to find out more about the bodies and items.

DID You Know?

Today, archaeologists are using cutting-edge forensic technology to bring the Maya back to life! More than 100 years ago, archaeologists visiting a Maya site took **plaster casts** of Maya artifacts they found. Today, Google and the British Museum in London have used the latest photographic technology to create digital images of these plaster models that can be studied on computers. Many of the precious objects are too fragile to hold, so seeing them on-screen allows scientists to study them safely. Anyone anywhere can now see these remains. This will make it easier for historians around the world to figure out what these objects were used for.

Skeletons and the soil around them can be tested by forensic scientists to find clues about the Maya and how they lived.

Forensic scientists can take an ancient skull, make a 3-D model of it on a computer, then recreate the dead person's face.

HOW SCIENCE SOLVED THE PAST:

MODELING MYSTERIES

We cannot visit the past, but we can model it. Forensic scientists use clues from ancient sites to figure out what the buildings that once stood there looked like. For example, **foundations** in the ground hint at walls. Pieces of pottery hint at garbage sites. Using this information, archaeologists work on a computer to create a **three-dimensional (3-D)** model of the site as it might once have been. This helps them learn how the buildings were made and what they might have been used for.

Forensic scientists can also use clues from the past to make 3-D models of people who lived long ago. They study skulls and skeletons to figure out what a person looked like. They then use that information to create a 3-D model of the person.

Raiding the Remains

Forensic scientists study skeletons or bodies to solve mysteries about a crime. They also study ancient remains to find out who people were and why they died. They can even use computers to create faces from skulls.

So what clues, or forensic footprints, did the Maya leave behind and what can we learn from them? Let's follow their forensic footprint trail!

WHAT LIES BENEATH?

In the past, archaeologists had to brave extreme heat, sharp, scratchy plants, and biting insects to explore the rain forest. When they discovered parts of ancient Maya cities, it was hard for them to figure out how big the cities really were. Today, that problem has been fixed thanks to science. Archaeologists use aerial **laser** technology called lidar to "see" beneath the jungle and explore the cities.

DID You Know?

The Maya built hundreds of miles of roads. Thanks to lidar, we can now see many of these roads from the sky. The Maya did not use their animals to carry things or pull carts, so the roads were not used to move goods from one place to another. The roads are raised above the ground, so people may have used them to get around in the rainy season, when the ground was very muddy. Experts once thought that people in Maya cities kept to themselves, but this new evidence suggests they were moving around between cities, and far more than we once thought.

Maya cities such as Ek Balam (meaning black jaguar) in Yucatan, Mexico, are often surrounded by thick jungle. Scientists can use lidar laser technology to find cities that are completely hidden.

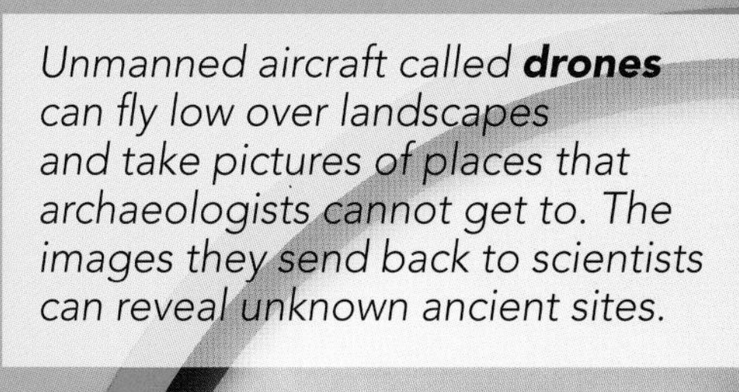

Unmanned aircraft called ***drones*** *can fly low over landscapes and take pictures of places that archaeologists cannot get to. The images they send back to scientists can reveal unknown ancient sites.*

This is a 3-D lidar image of part of the Maya city at Caracol in Belize. It took scientists just a few weeks to create this detailed map of 80 square miles (207 km²) of the site.

Looking with Lidar

Lidar devices shoot laser light at a target, then measure the time it takes for the light beams to bounce back. Forensic investigators use lidar to create realistic 3-D pictures of crime scenes, which they can use to find clues. Archaeologists attach lidar devices to drones or aircraft and fly them over the rain forest. The devices send laser light through tiny gaps in the trees. From this information, scientists create 3-D images of the land below that show where buildings were.

HOW SCIENCE SOLVED THE PAST:

EYE IN THE SKY

Historians learning about the Maya wondered if the jungle trees were hiding more than **monuments** or **temples,** in which no one had ever lived. Using powerful cameras in the sky, they were able to see into the thick jungle of the Petén region of Guatemala, a country in Central America. They found tens of thousands of stone platforms. On each of these platforms, a Maya house once stood. Historians were amazed to see this evidence. It showed that there were many more people living in the ancient Maya world than they had once thought.

VISITING CITIES

When archaeologists explore a Maya city on foot, they must hack their way through thick trees and bushes that cover the ancient walkways. The cities have become so overgrown that it is difficult to get a sense of what they looked like and how it must have felt to walk through them. This is now possible with the help of some amazing forensic technology.

Behind the Jungle

Forensic investigators use laser scanners and computers to "see inside" buildings. From this information, they create accurate 3-D pictures of areas inside buildings where crimes happened. Archaeologists use the same technology to look at 3-D pictures of Maya sites. This helps them better understand the layout of the cities and identify important buildings. The pictures also reveal that strong walls were built around Maya cities to protect them from attackers. This evidence has shown that the Maya were not a peaceful people, as early historians once believed!

DID You Know?

You, too, can walk the streets of a Maya city as though you were really there! In some law courts, people in the **jury** are given **virtual reality (VR)** headsets, so they can enter a 3-D animation of a crime scene. It allows them to "pick up" objects or examine a scene from different angles. Now, VR can help people explore Maya cities in incredible detail. As well as being great fun, it helps historians see things they might not have noticed before.

Wearing a VR headset to see a 3-D ***simulation*** *of a Maya city helps us explore how the Maya lived.*

In this ancient wall painting, a Maya man is playing a ball game. The Maya played ball games on huge stone courts. Thanks to 3-D images of ball courts, we can imagine what it was like to be there, playing the game!

HOW SCIENCE SOLVED THE PAST:

WHO HAS THE BEST VIEW?

Archaeologists in Nebraska created a 3-D picture of the ancient Maya city of Copán in Honduras. Archaeologists and historians looked at the picture on a computer to understand how the Maya designed their cities and how they lived in them. They discovered something surprising about the position of the houses in Copán. The richest, most important people in the city had a clear view of the temple that belonged to the city's ruler. However, most of the poorer people could not see the temple from their homes. This was probably so the important people could be reminded all the time that the ruler was much more powerful than them!

Historians can get a much clearer idea of life in Maya cities through 3-D virtual reality recreations of buildings, such as this temple.

MARKING TIME

One of the most important things archaeologists and anthropologists have to do is to find out how old ancient buildings and artifacts are. The style of pots and other objects the Maya made is a clue to their age. Sometimes objects have symbols on them that can date them. However, if there are no symbols and an object is in pieces, how can you tell its age?

Forensic Dating

Sometimes criminals try to sell a valuable object that they pretend is much older than it actually is. Forensic scientists can find out how old many artifacts are by using a technique called **carbon dating**. Most remains of once-living things, such as wood or bones, have a substance called **carbon** in them. Most carbon **decays** at a fixed rate, so if scientists measure how much carbon is left in an object they can put an age to it. For a long time, people wondered how goods such as salt and fish reached the Maya, who lived in inland cities. Forensic science helped solve this puzzle. Carbon dating of an ancient wooden paddle proved that the Maya used canoes to transport goods by river from the sea to their inland cities.

*Maya **hieroglyphs**, such as these from a Maya temple, are a form of writing. When the material they are carved into is carbon dated, it can give clues about when the writing was created.*

DID You Know?

The ancient Egyptians were not the only people who built **pyramids**—the Maya had them, too! Using the latest forensic carbon dating techniques, archaeologists have discovered a small pyramid that was built around 850 B.C.E., in a place called Ceibal in Guatemala. It is at least 200 years older than other Maya monuments found in the past.

HOW SCIENCE SOLVED THE PAST:

WHAT DAY IS IT?

For decades, experts puzzled over how they could figure out important dates in Maya history. Carvings showed that the Maya had a calendar, but no one knew the date on which it began. Using carbon dating, scientists tested a piece of wood from an ancient beam found in a Maya temple, which was carved with pictures of an important battle. Tests dated the beam to the end of the 7th century C.E. Now that they knew the date of the battle, historians could pinpoint other important events that shaped the Maya civilization.

The Maya calendar was made up of three circles or cycles. This is the Haab cycle, used to count 365 days in a year. The symbols around the edge are the 19 months—18 months of 20 days, one month of five days.

SIGNS IN BLOOD

When archaeologists find Maya pots, it can be hard to figure out what they were used for. Were they ancient soup bowls or storage pots—or were they used for something creepy? Forensic investigators can analyze tiny amounts of chemicals found on the inside of containers to discover what they were used for. This can help them discover if a murder victim was poisoned, for example. Could this forensic technique also help archaeologists studying the Maya?

Blood Bowls

Scientists were able to scrape tiny amounts of chemicals from the inside of some Maya pots they found. They analyzed the samples to determine what they were, and discovered blood! It turned out that the pots were specially made for collecting human blood. The ancient Maya had some gruesome ways to keep their gods happy. They cut people's skin using tools such as sharpened bone, stingray spines, and thorns, and collected the blood in bowls. They gave the blood as **offerings** to the gods. In return, the Maya asked for rain, good harvests, or success in battle.

Jaguars are the most dangerous of all animals in the rain forest. Sacrificing a jaguar was seen as a very powerful offering to the gods.

DID You Know?

The Maya also collected animal blood. Archaeologists tested traces of blood they found on black glass arrowheads (see next page), which they suspected the Maya used for **sacrifices**. They found both animal and human blood on the deadly weapons. They discovered that some of the unfortunate animals that the Maya killed as offerings to the gods included rodents, turkeys, and other birds. They also killed rabbits, and even big cats, such as jaguars!

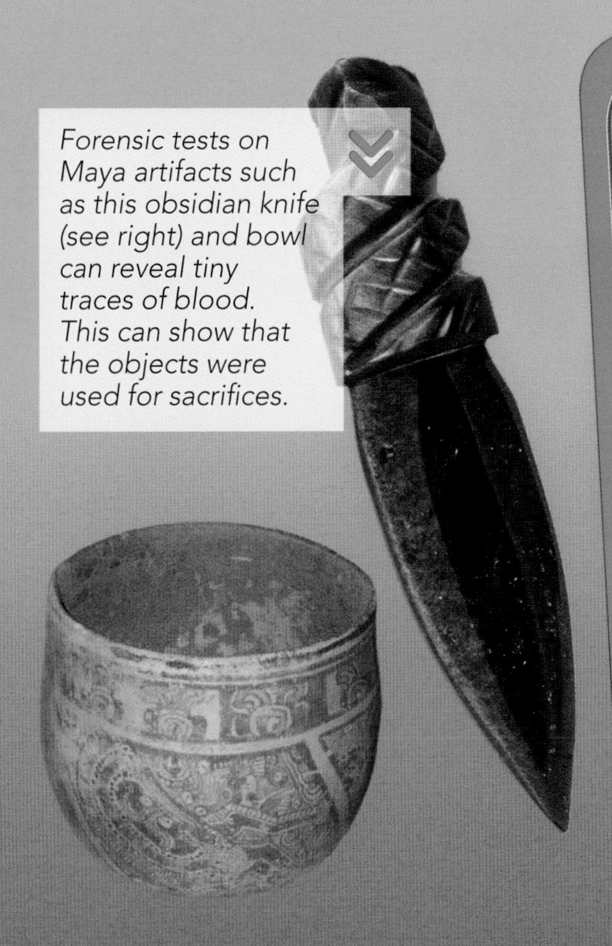

Forensic tests on Maya artifacts such as this obsidian knife (see right) and bowl can reveal tiny traces of blood. This can show that the objects were used for sacrifices.

HOW SCIENCE SOLVED THE PAST:

KITCHEN KNIVES OR BLADES FOR BLOOD?

Archaeologists searching through Maya sites found knives made from a black **volcanic** glass called obsidian. They wondered if these knives were used for **bloodletting.** But the knives showed no obvious signs of wear, so how could they prove it?

Forensic investigators use high-powered **microscopes** to spot traces of blood or signs of wear on weapons used in crimes such as murder. Archaeologists used high-powered microscopes to compare the wear on obsidian blades found in an ancient Maya cave in Belize, a small country in Central America, with wear on blades used to cut pig skin and bone. The tests showed that cutting different types of material, such as flesh or bone, caused different kinds of wear. The results showed that the Maya blades had probably been used for bloodletting.

This figure is called a Chacmool, which means "large red jaguar." A Chacmool is a carving of a person carrying offerings to the gods on a plate resting on its stomach. Forensic scientists can analyze the plate to see if it held blood.

THE MYSTERY OF MAYA BLUE

Blue was an important color for the Maya. They linked it to their rain god Chac. Some unlucky Maya would be painted blue and thrown down a well as a sacrifice to Chac! For the Maya, offerings of blood were vital to keep Chac happy—the Maya needed rain to water their corn crops. Historians have known for a long time that the Maya used blue because they have found it on many wall paintings and other objects. Scientists had also identified some of the substances used to make Maya blue. But how such a long-lasting, never-fading paint was made by the Maya was a mystery.

The natural wells that the Maya used for sacrifices were called cenotes. This is Ik-Kil cenote in Chichen Itza, Mexico. The water in Ik-Kil is a long drop of 85 feet (26 m) from the ground and more than 130 feet (40 m) deep. Archaeologists have found bones and jewelry in the spooky deep waters. Forensic scientists can analyze the bones to find out who was sacrificed in the well and when they died.

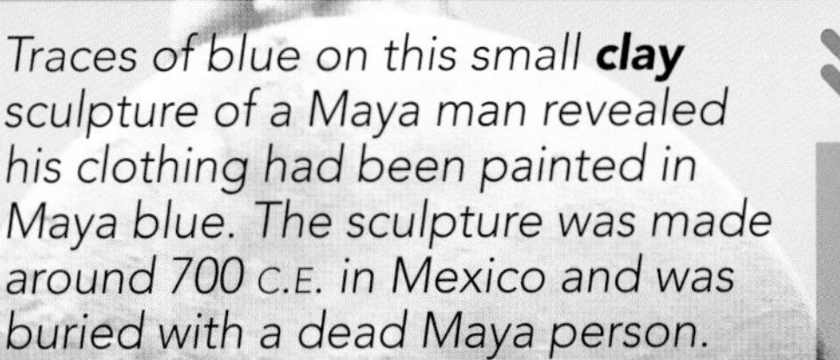

Traces of blue on this small ***clay*** *sculpture of a Maya man revealed his clothing had been painted in Maya blue. The sculpture was made around 700 C.E. in Mexico and was buried with a dead Maya person.*

HOW SCIENCE SOLVED THE PAST:

ADDED SPARKLE

The Maya used bright colors on their temples to make them dazzle in the sunlight. Forensic researchers in Australia analyzed tiny pieces of paint from the Maya city of Copan, using **infrared** light, which shows things that you cannot see in ordinary light. To their surprise, they found even tinier pieces of a **mineral** called mica mixed with the paint. When the sun shone, this mixture would have made the Maya buildings sparkle and glitter!

A Secret Ingredient

Now, forensic science has solved the puzzle. Forensic paint analysis is a technique investigators use on car paint and paint from clothing to find evidence of car theft and other crimes. Archaeologists have used forensic paint analysis to study Maya blue. Photograph scans taken by an extremely powerful microscope showed that it was probably heat and a secret ingredient—**resin** from the copal tree—that made it so special. The copal resin may have been the substance that allowed the color to stay so vibrant for so long.

DID You Know?

The Maya were smokers! Forensic scientists analyzed the chemicals in material that was still stuck to the inside of a 1,300-year-old pot. They found tiny amounts of tobacco—the earliest evidence that the Maya liked to smoke.

Forensic scientists discovered that copal resin (right) was the secret ingredient in the Maya blue color.

MAYA MURALS

HOW SCIENCE SOLVED THE PAST:

EVERYDAY LIFE

Most Maya murals show how the rich and powerful people, such as kings and priests, lived. This is important for historians, but they also want to know how the rest of the Maya lived.

At the ancient Maya city of Calakmul, archaeologists have found a painted pyramid decorated with murals that show ordinary Maya men, women, and children carrying and eating foods, and transporting other everyday goods. Forensic scientists are using special chemicals to preserve the murals and to reveal details that could not be seen before. This will tell us much about how ordinary Maya lived their daily lives—and what they looked like.

Much of what we know about the Maya comes from their grand paintings, called **murals**, which they left behind on the walls of temples and other buildings. Murals show important events in Maya history, such as battles and big parades. Some paintings are well preserved, but others have been worn away over time. Now, archaeologists are using forensic science to discover details in the paintings that only the Maya saw!

The murals discovered in the Maya city of Calakmul are very delicate. Forensic scientists are now able to preserve their paint by using special combinations of chemicals.

Seeing the Invisible

Forensic scientists have cameras that use infrared light to expose clues at crime scenes, such as bloodstains, that would otherwise be hidden. Archaeologists took pictures of murals at the ancient Maya site of Bonampak using powerful infrared light. They showed details that were invisible to the naked eye. The scientists used computers to build complete pictures of damaged paintings. The new pictures revealed hieroglyphs and images of gods and rulers carrying out different **rituals** that had not been seen for hundreds of years.

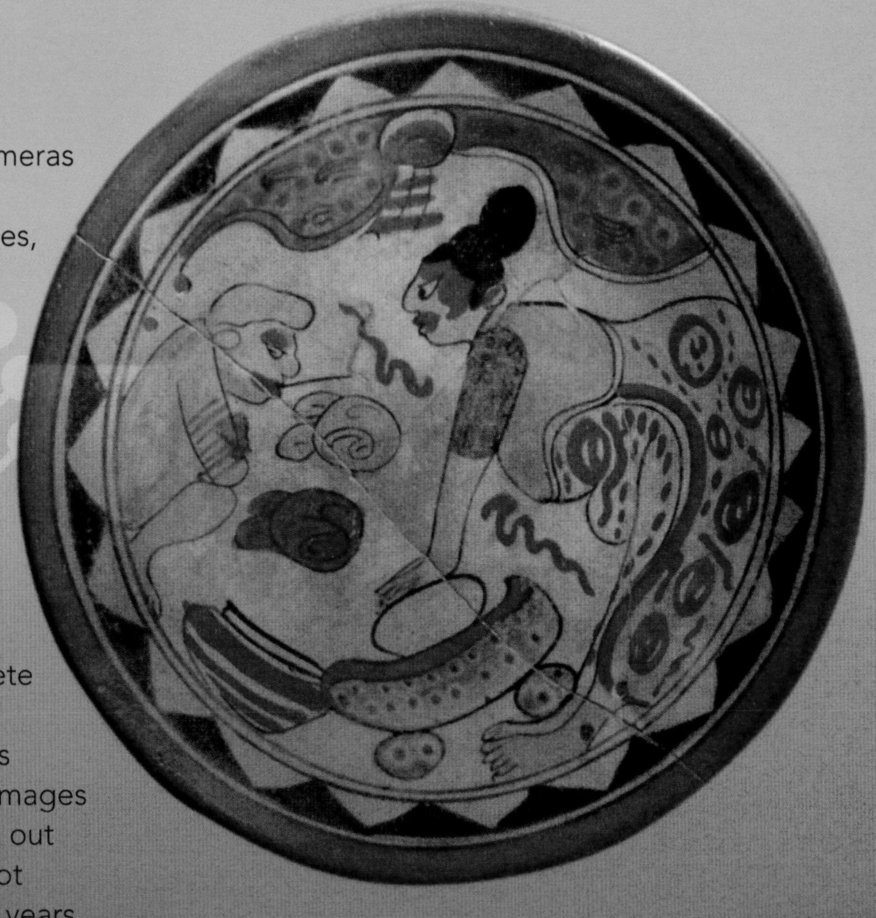

Maya paintings such as this one on a dish reveal many secrets about Maya lives. Here, a Maya woman is using a stone called a metate to grind cacao (see below).

DID You Know?

The Maya—and their gods—were chocolate lovers! Infrared cameras have revealed cloth bundles labeled with the Maya symbol for cacao, which is the bean used to make chocolate. Cacao beans were probably carried to temples as gifts for the gods.

The ancient Maya were the first people to use the seeds from cacao trees. They roasted the beans and ground them into powder (right). They mixed the powder with water and spices to make a bitter-tasting hot chocolate drink.

ON THE MENU

Some murals tell us what the Maya ate for dinner. They show people preparing food and even have hieroglyphs that tell us what some of the foods were. Historians wondered how the Maya organized themselves so that they could keep so many people fed. Thousands of people lived in Maya cities, so how did the Maya go about gathering and making enough food to feed them?

Forensic science can tell us more about what the Maya ate (see opposite). We know that maize, or corn, was an important food because many sculptures of the Maya maize god above have been found. The jewelry on his ears and head shows that he was a very important god.

Soil Studies

Forensic scientists can study the chemicals in the soil on a criminal's shoe treads to link that person to a crime scene. Scientists studying Maya sites look in the soil for high levels of a chemical called phosphorus, which is found in many foods. This can show them where the Maya prepared food. Scientists found phosphorus lining the edges of large, open Maya plazas, which are outdoor gathering places in the center of cities. This meant that large food markets had been held there. At the end of each market day, food remains were swept to the sides of the plazas. The discovery of the phosphorus was proof that Maya cities held large markets where people could buy their food.

DID You Know?

The Maya cooked their food with balls! Archaeologists discovered small clay balls when they dug up an ancient Maya kitchen. Forensic tests on the balls revealed tiny amounts of maize, bean, squash, and root crops. The balls were probably heated in a fire, then put into pots to heat food.

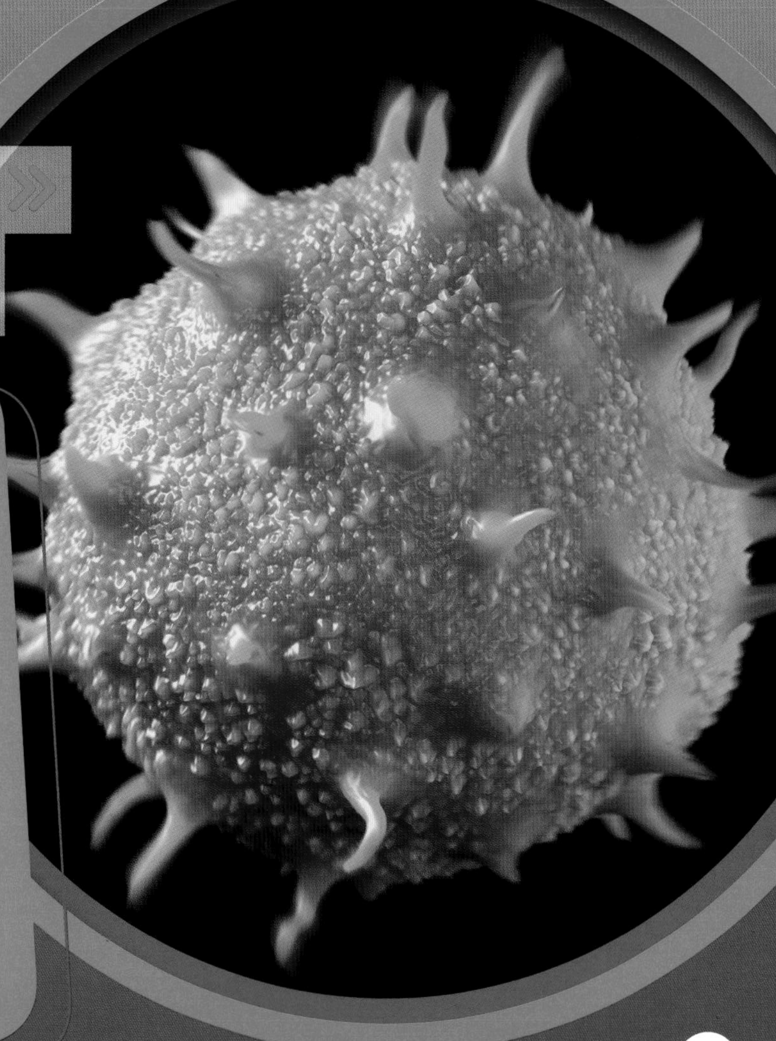

This is a tiny grain of sunflower pollen seen through a powerful microscope. Scientists can identify plants the Maya ate by examining pollen found at ancient Maya sites.

HOW SCIENCE SOLVED THE PAST:

TRACES IN THE TEETH

We know the Maya ate a lot of different foods, but what made up most of their diet? Scientists analyzing **plaque** remains on teeth from a Maya burial site discovered that the Maya diet included many more plant-based foods than originally thought. In fact, in some cases, 60 percent of the food they ate was maize! The studies also revealed that the Maya were talented cooks who used a wide variety of foods and spices.

SECRETS IN THE SKELETONS

The forensic study of bones and teeth can give clues about things such as what a victim of crime ate, where they lived, and how they died. The same forensic science can reveal some interesting Maya secrets, too. To understand more about the health and physical habits of the Maya people, scientists have forensically examined the remains of their bodies and the everyday objects they used.

HOW SCIENCE SOLVED THE PAST:

LEARNING FROM THE LEFTOVERS

Most of what we know of the Maya civilization is about Maya royalty, such as their big buildings, tombs, and customs. But most Maya were not royalty. How do we find out about them? Some of the answers can be found in what they left behind in their homes.

Archaeologists at the Florida Museum of Natural History used forensics to analyze 22,000 animal remains taken from Maya sites. They found that poor Maya villagers ate fish and shellfish from nearby rivers. They also found that in the cities, both the poor and the wealthy ate the same things—fish and shellfish from the sea and deer from the forests. People used to think that life was rough for ordinary Maya. This new evidence suggests they ate just as well as the rich, although the best cuts of meat from animals such as deer were probably just for the kings and priests.

DID You Know?

We know that the Maya kept dogs, cats, and turkeys. Scientists have examined the chemicals in animal bones from a 3,000-year-old Maya city called Ceibal and found that many of the animals ate maize. The maize was grown by the Maya and fed to the animals. Some dogs were kept as pets—others were eaten!

This is a Maya deer head mask from 600–900 C.E. Forensic analysis of animal bones has shown that deer were an important source of food for the Maya.

Forensic scientists analyze samples of bone or teeth to discover more about how a Maya person might have lived.

Buried Bones

The ancient Maya usually buried people in the floors of their houses, rather than in **cemeteries**. This may have been so they could stay close to their **ancestors**. Studying the skeletons can tell us much about the Maya. Bone analysis can tell us that most Maya people lived for 30 years. If they moved, the Maya dug up and reburied the bones of their ancestors under their new homes. This shows us that they believed their ancestors were still with them in some way and watched over them. It also shows that family life was important to the Maya.

MAYA MURDER MYSTERY

Archaeologists exploring the ancient Maya city of Cancuén in Guatemala in 2005 made a gruesome discovery. They found a jumble of 50 human skeletons. The victims had been killed, cut up, and placed inside a sacred pool. Had these people been killed as a sacrifice to the Maya gods? Or was there another reason for this brutal killing?

Identifying the Victims

DNA tests on the Maya skeletons revealed that most of the victims in the sacred pool were members of the same royal family. During a war with enemy Maya, the royal family's city was defeated. The enemies killed the royal family, cut them up, and threw them into the sacred pool. This kind of murder had not happened before in wars between the Maya. Some historians think that this increase in violence between rulers of neighboring cities may be one reason the Maya civilization came to an end.

Unlike the poor victims in the sacred pool, Maya royals were usually treated with great respect when they died. Often, their faces were covered in burial masks, such as this one.

DID You Know?

The Maya made human sacrifices underground. Deep in a cave in the jungle of Belize, archaeologists found many pots, stone figures, tools—and a skeleton (see page 25). Forensic analysis of the skeleton showed it was a 20-year-old Maya woman sacrificed more than 1,000 years ago. She is called the "Crystal Maiden" because her skeleton is covered in a glittery substance called calcite.

Over time, the skeleton of the "Crystal Maiden" has become stuck to the cave floor. To find her, archaeologists had to swim through a river 3 miles (5 km) long!

HOW SCIENCE SOLVED THE PAST:

THE LOST CHILDREN

The discovery of a king's burial chamber deep inside a Maya pyramid revealed treasures such as beautiful carvings, pots, and fabrics—but also the bones of six children! Were they members of the royal family, or was the truth more chilling?

Analysis of the skeletons revealed the six children were not related to the king and were most likely sacrificed at the time of his death. The anthropologists also determined that the children were very young when they died. As the Maya believed in life after death, the infants were probably sacrificed to help the king be reborn in the **afterlife**.

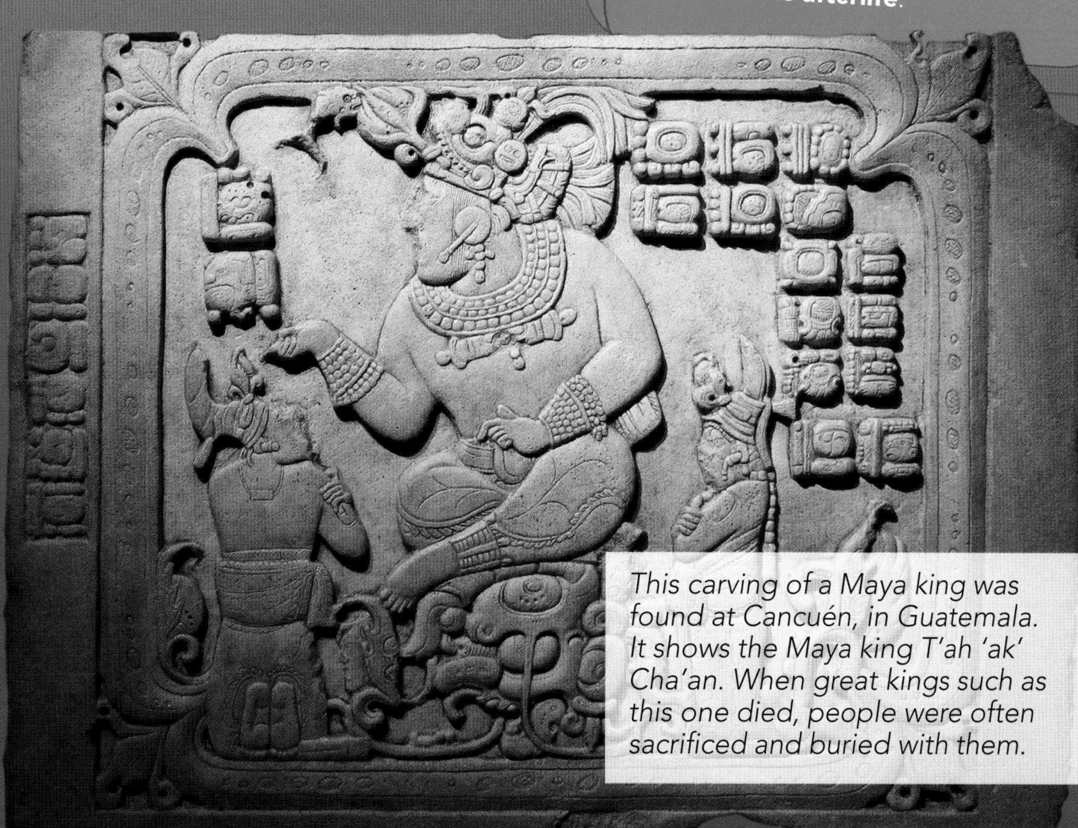

This carving of a Maya king was found at Cancuén, in Guatemala. It shows the Maya king T'ah 'ak' Cha'an. When great kings such as this one died, people were often sacrificed and buried with them.

WHERE DID THE MAYA GO?

For approximately 1,200 years, the cities of the Maya were thriving and powerful centers. Then, suddenly, all went quiet. Where did the Maya go? There is never only one cause for the end of a civilization. Wars between cities or the spread of a deadly disease may have helped bring about the Maya's downfall. Scientists have also discovered another possible explanation using forensic technology.

No More Forest Food?

Forensic experts use infrared light to discover hidden substances at crime scenes, such as ink and explosives. Archaeologists took infrared images from **satellites** high above Earth to find traces of a mineral called lime in Maya soil. The Maya used lime in their buildings. To help make enough lime for a small piece of wall 3 feet (1 m) high and 3 feet (1 m) wide, the Maya had to burn 20 big trees. The large amount of lime shown in the infrared images tells us the Maya must have chopped down many forests. This is called **deforestation**. Without the trees and their roots to hold the ground together, the top layer of soil would have blown away or been washed away by rain. This would have made it much harder for the Maya to grow enough food. Many people may have starved to death.

« *As their civilization grew, the Maya needed bigger cities. To make room for them, did the Maya cut down forests to clear land, which they then built on? Infrared pictures taken above Maya sites show that the Maya must have cut down huge areas of forest, then built on that land.*

HOW SCIENCE SOLVED THE PAST:

DID THE MAYA WORLD DRY UP?

Could the Maya habit of cutting down trees also have made a **drought** worse? Forensic investigators use computer simulations to recreate crime scenes that change over a period of time, such as the buildup to a terrorist attack. Archaeologists use computer simulations and models to see how temperatures increased and rainfall reduced as the Maya cut down their forests. In the rain forest, trees help soak up heat and make rain. Maya deforestation would have caused the land to dry up and the plants to die, leading to severe food shortages.

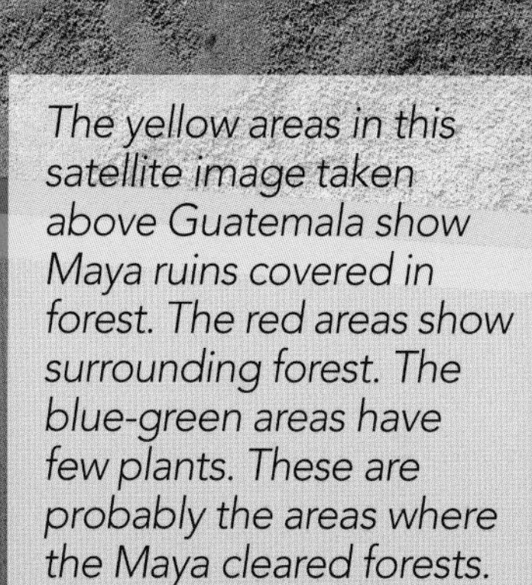

The yellow areas in this satellite image taken above Guatemala show Maya ruins covered in forest. The red areas show surrounding forest. The blue-green areas have few plants. These are probably the areas where the Maya cleared forests.

Forensic science has helped prove that the Maya did not die out altogether. People living in Yucatan, Mexico, today are the descendants of the amazing ancient Maya.

DID You Know?

Not all the ancient Maya died out. There are still around 6 million Maya alive today! DNA studies can prove that many people in Mexico and Central America are related to the ancient Maya. This suggests that as Maya cities struggled to feed their populations, some people lost faith in their rulers and left to build new farms and lives elsewhere.

FORENSIC FUTURE

We may never know all of the exact details of how the Maya lived, but forensic science techniques are helping us learn more than we ever dreamed possible. From lidar mapping and chemical analysis to infrared and satellite images, forensic technology is helping us find clues that we never knew existed.

What might forensic technology uncover in the future? Technology is a gateway to the past. Our picture of the ancient Maya is becoming clearer with every tiny piece of the puzzle that is discovered and fitted into place!

DID You Know?

The Maya believed that caves, tunnels, and natural **sinkholes** in the ground were doorways into the world of the gods! Forensic investigators use **sonar** to search for bodies and weapons underwater. In the future, archaeologists will be able to explore flooded caves using sonar and **radar.** They will see into hidden passageways and chambers to find artifacts such as skeletons of people who were killed as sacrifices. This will help historians understand more about the ancient Maya and their fascinating beliefs.

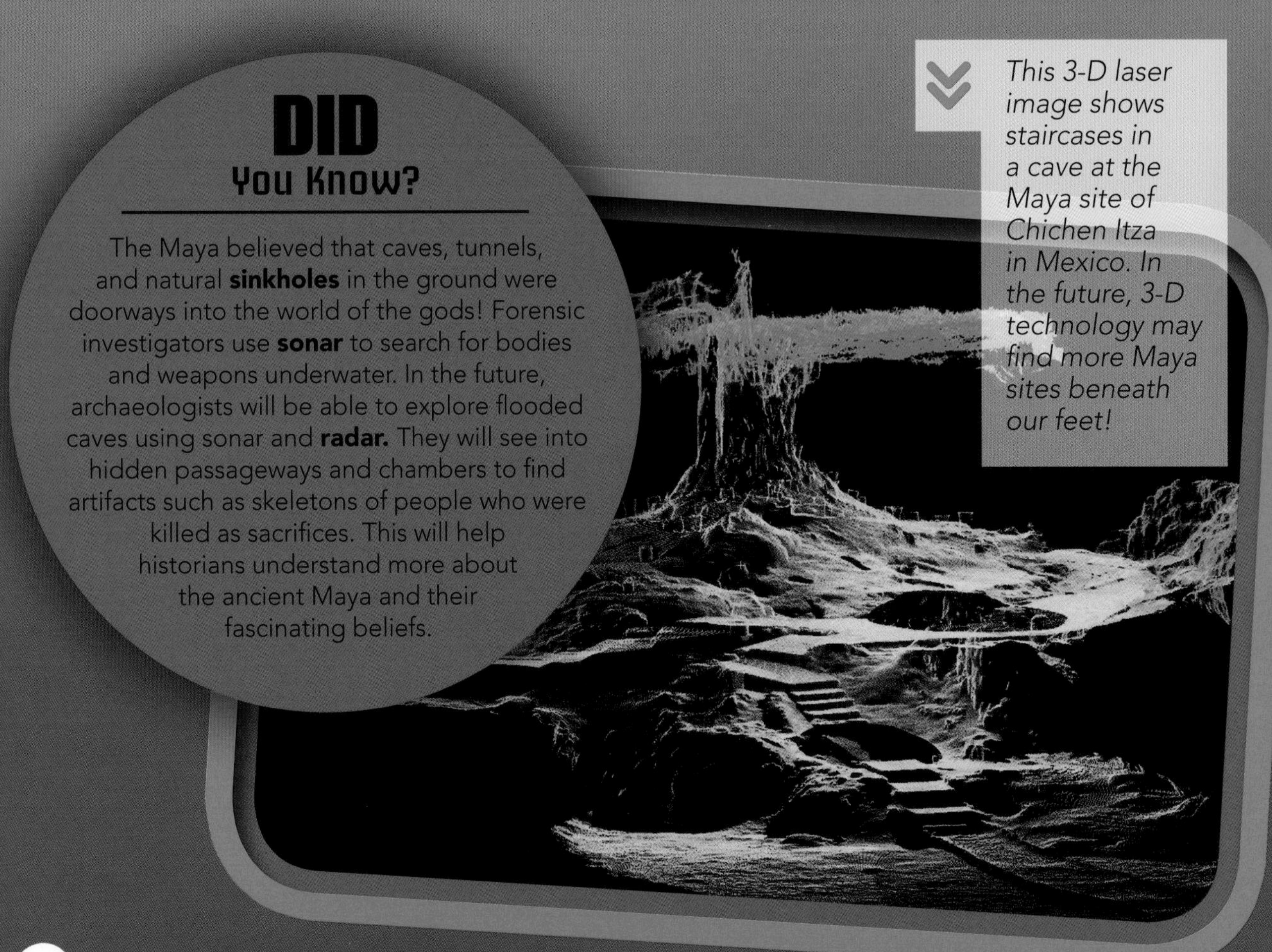

This 3-D laser image shows staircases in a cave at the Maya site of Chichen Itza in Mexico. In the future, 3-D technology may find more Maya sites beneath our feet!

CAN FORENSICS SOLVE...?

Here are two of the great still-unsolved mysteries about the ancient Maya civilization. Researchers, historians, and archaeologists will need great forensic science techniques to solve these mysteries!

Great Maya Disappearing Act

Why did the Maya leave their cities in around 900 C.E.? There are a number of theories, including drought, food shortages, wars, and disease. But no one knows for sure what caused a great civilization to end so quickly. Forensic scientists will try to solve the mysteries by using carbon dating, chemical analysis, and other techniques on Maya artifacts. With the help of forensic science, one day, scientists may be able to say once and for all what events caused the collapse of the Maya.

Super Smart

The Maya were very advanced in building techniques, science, and technology. They also seemed to know a lot about **astronomy**. How did they get this knowledge, or figure it out, deep in the jungle and far from other civilizations? One way archaeologists may solve the mystery is by forensic examination of pieces of Maya text. New technology may reveal words and ideas that explain why the Maya were so advanced.

GLOSSARY

Please note: Some **bold-faced** words are defined where they appear in the book.

afterlife Life after death
analyze Study something carefully
ancestors Relatives who died long ago
anthropologists Experts who study who ancient people were, how they lived, and where they came from
archaeologists Experts who study where ancient people lived and the things they left behind
astronomy The study of the planets, stars, and other objects in space
bloodletting Making a person or an animal bleed as part of a religious ceremony
carbon A chemical found in all living plants and animals
carbon dating A technique used to find out the age of an object
cemeteries Large burial grounds
civilization A settled and stable community in which people live together peacefully and use systems such as writing to communicate
clay A heavy, sticky material that can be shaped easily and becomes hard when baked
decays Rots
deforestation Clearing a wide area of forest
DNA Material that contains all of the information needed to create an individual living thing
drones Unmanned aircraft guided by remote control or onboard computers
drought Period of time when there is so little rain that plants die
evidence Facts and information that tell us if something is true
forensic science The use of scientific methods and techniques to find clues about crimes or the past
foundations Solid structures that support a building from underneath
hieroglyphs Pictures or symbols that represent words, parts of words, or sounds
infrared A type of light that feels warm but cannot be seen
jury A group of people in a courtroom who make a decision about a legal case
laser A very narrow, highly concentrated beam of light
microscopes Devices used to see objects that are too small to be seen by the naked eye
mineral A solid substance found naturally on Earth that makes up rocks
monuments Statues, buildings, or other structures made to remember an event, a time, or a person
murals Wall paintings
offerings Things that people give as part of a religious ceremony or ritual
plaque A sticky layer that builds up on teeth
plaster casts Copies of objects made from a paste that becomes hard when it dries
preserve Make sure something remains the same
pyramids Large structures built with a square base and four triangular sides meeting at a point at the top
radar A system that uses invisible radio waves to find the position of objects we cannot see
rain forest A thick forest of tall trees found in tropical areas where there is usually a lot of rain
remains Bodies, bones, objects, or parts of objects left over from the past
resin A sticky substance produced by some trees
rituals Ceremonies performed for religious reasons
sacred Something that is special or important to a religion
sacrifices Killings carried out to honor a god or gods
satellites Machines in orbit around Earth that collect information or are used for communication

simulation Something made to look like something else so it can be studied more closely

sinkholes Holes in the ground that are usually caused by underground water

sites Places where something is or was

sonar A device that uses sound waves to "see" under the water

symbols Images that represent something else

techniques Methods of doing particular tasks

temples Buildings where people go to worship their god or gods

three-dimensional (3-D) Having or appearing to have length, width, and depth

virtual reality (VR) A 3-D, computer-generated world that can be explored by a person

volcanic Produced by a volcano

LEARNING MORE

Books

Honders, Christine. *Ancient Maya Culture* (Spotlight on the Maya, Aztec, and Inca Civilizations). PowerKids Press, 2016.

Roman, Carole P. *If You Were Me and Lived In … The Mayan Empire.* Chelshire, Inc., 2017.

Stoltman, Joan. *Looking for Clues with a Detective* (Get to Work!). Gareth Stevens, 2018.

Stuckey, Rachel. *Ancient Maya Inside Out* (Ancient Worlds Inside Out), Crabtree Publishing Company, 2017.

Websites

www.ducksters.com/history/maya/daily_life.php
Try the Ducksters education site for information on Maya daily life—and much more.

www.explainthatstuff.com/forensicscience.html
Take a look if you want to know more about forensic science and how it is used at crime scenes.

https://maya.nmai.si.edu/maya
The Smithsonian National Museum of the American Indian introduces lots of information about the world of the Maya.

www.nationalgeographic.org/topics/maya
Find facts and videos about ancient Maya culture on this National Geographic site.

INDEX

About the Author

Louise Spilsbury loves researching new information on a wide variety of subjects. She has written more than 200 books, some co-authored with her husband Richard, on a range of topics from art and ants to zippers and zoos!